ENABLER'S JOURNEY DETACHMENT

Enabler's Journey Recovery Series
Book Two

Angie G Meadows MS, RN; Perry Meadows MD, JD; & Sarah Meadows BS

Abstract This book empowers us to learn survival skills with 12 DETACHMENT PRINCIPLES. *The spiraling financial consequences, mental anguish, emotional chaos, and physical drain of enabling begs the voice of detachment to ensure self-preservation.* **This book is a useful tool in dealing with individuals with Substance Use Disorder, alcoholics, abusers, or irresponsible adults in our lives.** It includes many self-assessment tools: Entitlement Evaluation, Empowerment Plan, Helpless Trap, Healthier Me, Healthy Speech Evaluation, Negative Emotional Triggers, Unmet Needs, Obsessive Thinking Traps, Forgiveness, Bitterness, Reconciliation, Holidays, Suffering, Power to Stop Enabling, Self-talk, Rules for Survival, Emotional Separation, Healthy Separation, Unhealthy Ways of Caring vs. Healthy Ways of Caring, Heart Evaluation, Goal setting, Higher and Lower Levels of Love, True and False Recovery, Entanglement Gauge, Trust Scale Guide, Relationship Goals, the Detachment Quick Guide and practical steps, reflective thinking, and self-evaluation tools.

A Thousand Tears, LLC
PO Box 561
Lewisburg, PA 17837
enablersjourney@gmail.com
www.enablersjourney.com

This book is intended as general information only and should not be used to diagnose or treat any health condition. Considering the complex, individual, and specific nature of health problems, this book is not intended to replace professional medical advice. The ideas, procedures, and suggestions in this book are intended to supplement, not replace, the advice of a trained medical professional. Consult your physician before adopting any of the suggestions in this book, as well as about any condition that may require diagnosis or medical attention. The author and publisher disclaim any liability arising directly or indirectly from the use of this book.

This publication is designed to provide accurate and authoritative information regarding the subject matter covered. It is sold with the understanding that the publisher is not engaged in rendering legal, accounting, or other professional advice. If legal advice or other expert assistance is required, the services of a competent professional person should be sought.

From a *Declaration of Principles* jointly adopted by a Committee of the American Bar Association and a Committee of Publishers and Associations.

DEDICATION

To all who are suffering with Enabling Behaviors
May you recover your life.

Contents

FORWARD

The individual with Substance Use Disorder's maelstrom threatens to capture family and friends into a violent, tightening orbit of its vortex. The fight to extricate oneself is often a lonely journey made more difficult because of pity that is both intrinsic and extrinsic in origin as the loved one is often a virtuoso at plucking heartstrings. One may suffer reproach from the addicted love one as well as from others caught in an enabler's orbital.

This workbook is a guide toward a therapeutic detachment. The successful implementation of these measures will serve to restore and preserve the health and well-being of you and your family. It will also lay the groundwork toward a more rational and healthy relationship with a person with Substance Use Disorder.

We and too many others are on this journey. You are not alone.

--Bret Yarczower, MD

INTRODUCTION

Healthy detachment leads to healthy connectedness. Genuinely strong and vibrant relationships develop from relationship interdependency. Dominance, control, clinging or passivity leaves us empty, lonely and confused. Having a progressive journey to health and well-being includes identifying the bad and separating it from the good. We can then consciously choose to detach from the vile and have the energy to invest in what is precious.

This workbook is excerpted and expanded from our book titled: "A Thousand Tears: An Enabler's Journey". The book is available on Amazon.com. The Christian version of the book is called: "An Enabler's Journey: A Christian Perspective." The first book in this series is Enabler's Journey Recovery Plan which assist an individual to develop an enabler's recovery plan with accountability questions, self-care plan, and healthy coping skills. It also discusses how to identify the methods people with Substance Use Disorder (SUD) use to deceive new enablers or pretend recovery. The true/false recovery outline is also included in this book. It helps us understand the depth of character needed for long-term recovery.

Consider all this information and use your best judgment to determine what works for you. Only you can identify what does and does not apply to your circumstances. This book is not meant to give counsel, but to give insight into your own thinking or behaviors and to allow you to determine what thinking or behaviors are or are not serving you well.

I use he/him to refer to the person with addictive behaviors. You may use whatever gender pronoun applies to your situation.

I use the words "Substance Use Disorder" (SUD) to refer to our loved ones caught in any addictive behaviors. This could include the strongest street drugs, prescription medications, excessive use of alcohol, gambling, pornography, gaming, food addictions and a myriad of other things that may control our lives. This is not meant to be a negative term, but an inclusive term to refer to those with dysfunctional coping behaviors. This can include us and our addictive enabling behaviors.

Although this book is based upon our experience with people exhibiting substance use disorder, the principles also apply to those caught in domestic violence and with other addictive behaviors.

The main writer is Angie. My constant coaches and editors are Perry and Sarah. When we were enabling our loved ones, we were going financially deeper and deeper in debt. We had to admit that no amount of money could ever solve the deep-seated issues of addiction in our loved one. We had no choice but to stop or to drown financially. We had to seek our own recovery from people and circumstances we could not change or control. Watching our loved ones suffer with addiction and enabling behaviors can be unbearable at times.

Detachment is an emotional developmental maturity skill. Detachment gives others the permission to own their decisions and consequences derived from those decisions. Detachment allows me to have a better day.

It is our desire to assist you to convert the sorrows of enabling into steadfast stability. May you have the courage to recover your life and find your joy.

PRINCIPLE #1

Detachment in love without fear

Detachment is not cold, withdrawn or isolated, but a decision to do what is best for myself first. It is a healthy boundary of knowing where my responsibility begins and where it ends. It is a healthy separation that leads to healthy connectedness.

It will be obvious when I have done this because I will stop trying to control others and start recognizing my own physical and emotional needs: tired, hungry, angry, lonely, etc.

PRACTICAL STEPS

1. **Step back from the insanity.** Anyone who is out of control emotionally is not safe. This person is in an emotionally exaggerated mode characterized by excessive complaining. This type of complaining can escalate quickly into raging.
2. **Leave the room when emotions are high.** When a person is emotionally or physically out of control, there isn't anything you can do to appease them. Remove yourself from their presence as quickly as possible.
3. **Don't argue or talk with someone who isn't sober.** An intoxicated person repeats themselves incessantly. Whatever they are

repeating is usually something from their past they haven't dealt with properly and released. It can be as devastating as trauma from war, unresolved pain from a past divorce or a simple nagging irritation.

4. **Refuse to be provoked.** If you allow yourself to become angry, the immature person in front of you will mirror your response. Unfortunately, they will most likely power up and exaggerate the behavior. Don't allow anyone to engage you who isn't in control of their emotions or behaviors.

5. **Don't take abusive words as truth or internalize them.** This takes practice. It is an **emotional maturity skill** that must be developed. Abusive words sting. Unkind or careless words can alter your mood and rob you of your peace.

6. **When it is the other person's emotional pain, let them own it.** It is important for others to feel their own pain. There are times to comfort them. Sometimes we can guide others through questions to acknowledge where their pain originated and why this situation triggered an exaggerated emotion. Hopefully, the original emotional wound can be uncovered and empower the person to release the pain that causes them to be stuck emotionally.

7. **Allow yourself to identify and feel all your emotions.** *Move through emotions quickly.* This is another **emotional maturity skill** that can be cultivated. Do this by visualizing the emotion outside of yourself. Observe the emotion as separate from you. Do not identify with emotions. Say to yourself, "Yes, I am sad. I feel depressed, but the emotions aren't me. They are just emotions."

8. **Don't think of yourself as an emotion, but as stability.** An example is fear vs. courage. Identify who you want to be inside: I am strong and courageous. I am peaceful. I am free from anxiety. I am loved. *Don't let emotions drive your thinking. Thinking guides behaviors.*

9. **Understand most people will not change without suffering.** Suffering, for some, can be a good motivator for change. They need it. Do not rescue them from consequences of poor choices. The more irresponsible a person is with their decisions in life, the tougher the consequence will need to be for them to learn to become responsible. When they bring their problems and attempt to coerce you to correct the problem or pay the fine, ask: "What did you do to receive this consequence? What could you have done differently? What have you learned from this experience?"

10. **A person making absurd decisions need the consequences of their poor choices to change their behaviors.** If you or I usurp the consequence, we have robbed them of a *life lesson*. It is like helping a butterfly out of a cocoon. His wings will be weak and never fly. Our loved ones need struggles to mature and grow strong. Prison may save their lives. A DUI may wake them up and save someone else's life. If you rescue a person with (SUD), you almost always guarantee the need for another life lesson with stronger consequences. Their behaviors may progress from failing grades, falsifying worker's compensation claims, robbing employers or other employees to bank fraud or armed robbery. Consequences may progress from fees, fines, 30-day jail time to life-threatening overdoses.

Let them learn while the consequences are minor. It is better for them to lose their license for a year and have forced accountability with court-ordered probation than to spend ten years in prison for vehicular manslaughter. Any life- threatening behaviors need to be addressed immediately. Any lying, cheating or stealing should not be tolerated.

An a person with SUD in partial recovery, isn't in recovery.

PRINCIPLE #2

Detachment brings peace

Detachment is not caring less; but, caring more for my emotional stability. If I make *emotional stability my goal*, I need to be aware of my instability or imbalance and develop a structured plan to rebalance myself.

ASK YOURSELF

- **Is it my problem?** If I allow my emotions to be involved, I will become an easy target for manipulation or an impulsive decision.
- **Is it my responsibility?** It is important to place the responsibility for another person's problem squarely upon their shoulders.
- **Is it a consequence to a poor choice?** Poor decisions beget poor outcomes. When consequences are excruciating, it is time to seize the opportunity and allow it to motivate your loved one to seek outside help by going to a counselor, support group or rehabilitation center. Lead the way and work *Enabler's Journey Recovery Plan*.
- **Is it a consequence of defiance, rebellion or breaking the law?** Coddling defiance, rebellion or law breaking with "excuse making" guarantees an *entitled* loved one will be justified in continuing a path of destruction. *Entitlement is a belief that we deserve privileges we have not earned.*

ENTITLEMENT EVALUATION

SKEWED BEHAVIORS

- Discontent
- Greedy
- Nothing pleases them except momentarily
- Focused on temporal issues
- Finds Fault
- What's mine is mine and what's yours is mine.
- Lazy in housework, yardwork or childcare
- Impulsive speech
- Impulsive negative behaviors
- Demanding in relationships
- Developmentally an adult adolescent...argues with authority figures.

POOR CHARACTER DEVELOPMENT

- Complainer
- Selfish
- Angry
- Easily irritated or impatient
- Blames others for their problems. No personal responsibility accepted.
- Cheats, lies and steals

MATERIAL POSSESSION SKEWEDNESS

- Possessive about material objects.
- Careless in taking care of personal belongings.

• Destructive with property.
• Thinks others property is for their use.
• Frivolous impulsive spending
WORK ETHIC DEFICIENCIES
• Demands things they haven't worked to earn.
• No amount of income is enough.
• Doesn't want to serve others or give of their time.
• Thinks others owe them something.
• Think they are worth more of an hourly wage without credentials.
• Doesn't see menial jobs as steppingstones to develop character and a work ethic.
• They do the minimal amount of required work at the lowest standard.
• Thinks the government owes them something.
• Demands the best quality healthcare without paying premiums or being compliant with treatment and then complains about the care.

Who are my emotionally unbiased counselors? As enablers, it is difficult to see the forest for the trees. We also need counseling and support groups. We need to seek out trusted friends and family who can guide us to make emotionally unbiased decisions based upon long-term goals.

Is this person exhibiting self-destructive behaviors that have deep roots? Perhaps your loved one was abandoned or neglected. Maybe there was a divorce or another unstable environment in childhood. These wounds need to be addressed and healed. If you caused a wound, repent quickly and often and then return their present and future decision-making responsibilities back to them.

Are there children who need nurtured or protected? Many decisions to enable others are for the benefit of the children caught in the middle. If you decide to assist for the sake of the children, *plan well*. Go the extra mile to assure your money is not embezzled from you on false pretenses. Go to the pharmacy and buy the medicine. Go to the thrift store and buy the clothing. (New clothing may be sold to resell shops for drug money.) Buy the shoes for the child. Address an envelope and send the child support to the correct authorities for the child. (Only consider this if they are seriously working a recovery plan, not for the parent who has squandered their wages.) Make any financial support conditional and temporary. It is vital that the person with SUD does not receive any cash.

Cash can be an enormous temptation to slide back into old habits.

ENMESHMENT

Am I enmeshed? *The definition of Enmeshment is to be entangled or wrapped up in a net.*

Enablers can become so enmeshed that other adults have developed a lifestyle of dependency. If this has happened, disentangle gently. For example, say, "Next month you can pay for your phone or switch to an affordable pre-pay phone." Then say, "The next month, let's plan on you paying utilities." Continue a verbal and written plan of progressive independence with your loved one. Attempt to become completely disentangled within a year. You shouldn't be responsible for child support, rent, utilities, phones, cable, car insurance or car repairs for healthy, independent working adults.

Think seriously about how you are going to approach this subject. If you start with irritation, you will not like their response. If you start the conversation with repentance for usurping their independence and their confidence to become functioning adults, you can develop an *"Empowerment Plan"* to help them succeed.

EMPOWERMENT PLAN

Plan	Date	Outcome
BASIC		
Phone		
Child Support/Day Care		
Utilities		
Rent		
Car payment		
ADVANCED		
Car Insurance		
Health Insurance		
Car Repairs		
Medication		
Dental needs		
SUPERLATIVE		
Vacations		
Dining out		
Clothing		
Cigarettes or other non-essentials		

Cable, internet or other luxury expenses		

Develop a gradual plan with an actively recovering person with SUD to stop financial support. *Those in active addiction are to obtain **no** financial support until they are ready to be responsible and work a recovery plan.* Occasionally, the <u>no financial support plan</u> for an active substance user needs to be altered if antibiotics or life-saving medicine is needed. But you cannot give them cash.

These financial independence goals will give them confidence to manage their lives. Let them know any financial assistance comes with accountability. It is a leg-up and not a handout.

Superlative category is for financial wants. If you see your loved one spending in these areas and neglecting financial responsibilities, let them suffer the electric turned off and work to pay for it to be reconnected.

The consequences and suffering of poor financial decisions will give them motivation to budget, plan better, and develop self-control. Living in poverty can be a great motivator to work, develop employable skills, or educate themselves better to increase income.

If they are living in your basement and can afford to smoke cigarettes or marijuana, rent movies, and go to concerts, they have money to help with the bills or pay their own rent somewhere else. It's a matter of growing up and setting adult priorities. All financial assistance requires accountability.

| Expect them to hoist themselves up into the saddle of life and progress.

Your loved ones may have developed a lifestyle based upon your support and may need to lower their monthly expenses by adjusting their expectations. The sooner they do this, the less resentful they will be as you disentangle yourself. Healthy and responsible adults desire to be independent from parents and grandparents. They will also show caretaking behaviors towards children, infirmed or elderly. They will not embezzle money with false pretenses of emergency needs.

They may need to develop a plan to obtain employable skills. Community College, Certifications, or Apprenticeships can be key to improving income.

Responsible college students with successful grades will need assistance. If you are financially assisting them, demand an accounting of their finances if you suspect it is being squandered. Help them to develop a financial budget.

FREEDOM TO BE HAPPY WHEN OTHERS ARE DEPRESSED

- Remember the butterfly struggles? These daily ups and downs are normal and necessary.
- **Do not** take on their problems. Listen with sympathy. Then take a deep breath and say, "What are **you** going to do about it? How are **you** going to plan so you don't end up with this problem again?
- **Do not** listen to grumbling, whining and complaining, but encourage problem solving. These negative verbal embellishments offer little and incite helplessness.
- Instead, guide them to develop a plan to succeed or they may end up in a *helpless trap*.

HELPLESS TRAP

VICTIM THINKING	DISCIPLINED THINKING
Victim mentality (whining, complaining)	Disciplining my mind to change thinking patterns

Poor planning	Plan and prepare for change
Unpredictable circumstances	Flexible, expect the unexpected and make allowances for it
Blaming	Accepting responsibility for my actions
Excuse making	No excuses
All or nothing thinking	Balance
Fainthearted (giving up too quickly)	Steadfast and diligent
Fearful	Courageous
Anxious	Confident
Stressed	Relaxed
Constant worry	Trusting
Insomnia	Resting
Overeating	Disciplined eating
Under eating/anorexic	Healthy meals
Self-abuse (cutting, mind altering behaviors, gaming, binge television, irresponsible actions, lacking self-care etc.)	Self-care (exercise, healthy diet, healthy thinking, counseling if needed, community of caring friends)
I will never be better	I can do this!
Nothing will ever help me	I can be patient while I search for answers
I will never overcome this injury, illness, addiction or diagnosis	I can improve in many areas, and keep working and be hopeful with stubborn issues
I am hopeless	I am full of hope
I feel like giving up	No retreat

Frequently have feelings of depression	Empowered through disciplining my thinking and separating my identity from my irrational thinking
Suicidal thinking	Suicidal thinking isn't an option. I refuse to go there.

Sometimes, we can have the answer in our hands. We know what to do, but we do not understand how to implement the changes needed. For example, if we have a chronic illness, there is so much new information that can help us naturally heal our bodies. But if we think of ourselves as chronically sick, we may give up and stop searching for answers. This creates a helpless trap. Hope brings healing within our grasp.

The answers will become clear to us as we settle ourselves and slow down. Researching our problem for a hundred hours and trying a hundred things develops perseverance. If none of them work, more time may be needed, or a slower progress may be more realistic. We may have discovered a hundred things that don't work. The things that I tried ten years ago didn't work. Now with more information, teaching, dedication and perseverance, they are working. Just don't give up. Don't lose hope.

Turn a helpless/victim mentality into a *life lesson of maturity*. *Victim mentality causes us suffering*. Recognize this helpless thinking and refuse it. It only leads to more suffering.

It is a simple shift. Not easy, but simple. I can work my own recovery plan to empower myself not to be a victim. As much as I would like to do it, I cannot break through the mental blockage of someone else's *helpless trap*. I can help them develop a plan, but they must set up accountability. They may have to be sick of suffering to be motivated for lasting change.

If we give our loved ones the tools to change their thinking, we can wait for them to be sick of suffering and ready to do the work change requires. Sometimes, it takes a decade before they move towards change.

We can stop our whine. We can lead the way. If we show them health and emotional stability is within our grasp, our loved ones may follow and pursue health and well-being.

> Enabling others to be comfortable in addiction or illness will not give them the hope to propel forward to seek improvement or change.

CHANGE OUR THINKING

- Refuse all foolish thoughts.
- Refuse to worry about things we can't control.
- Refuse to be stressed over someone else's problem.
- Refuse to fret over things that haven't happened as if they were happening now.
- Detach and disentangle from those who dominate, control, rob and abuse you.
- Detach from the memories of past trauma.
- Attach to the good memories and hold them dear.

Identify false thinking patterns. Empower yourself by refusing them and discipline yourself in healthy thinking skills. Meditate on healthy thoughts. Mentally role play healthy change and how it could improve your life.

What changes are you ready to pursue? Discuss the following goals with your loved one for their active recovery? Empower them to develop a plan to meet goals. When they see these goals, they will understand the work they need to do to maintain sobriety and safe relationships.

> Recovery is intentional.

GOAL SETTING

Immediate Goals	Date	Outcome
In-patient treatment center		
Day/Evening recovery program		
Support group meeting (4-5 a week during early recovery)		
Support group meetings (2-3 a week for a year)		
Sponsor, accountability partners		
Employment		
Paying Child-support,		
Being Responsible for Warrants, court fees or fines		
Intermediate Goals		
Phone, bus pass		
Car, insurance		
Paying for food		
Paying rent for a bedroom, basement, or sober living facility		
Recognizing and changing any false thinking		
Long Term Goals		

Support group meeting (1-2 a week for life to give back to others in need of support)		
Courage to face life sober		
Courage to ask for help when needed		

Enabling and coddling leads to a life of dependency and frustration.

Mature, unemotional goal setting can help launch your loved one into responsible adulthood and a better life. Set a boundary on your time, energy, finances, and assistance. Demand respect of boundaries.

If your loved one will not work a plan or is unable to follow through, he may need more accountability from others who aren't sympathetic to his emotional pleas. He may need time in prison to sober up and desire recovery.

An enabler is not likely strong enough to hold a beloved family member accountable. This is done by someone who can stick to a plan and not be manipulated emotionally.

As an enabler, it was my tendency to **emotionally manipulate** the responsible person who was developing a plan for my loved one in active addiction. In my *active enabling* days, I have been known to manipulate judges, probation officers, counselors, and sponsors. Trust me, this doesn't work.

Manipulation to remove consequences only necessitates the need for more consequences which will be too big for an enabler to usurp.

As a recovering enabler, I was not able to set up boundaries with my loved one with SUD that would be respected. *A "hands off" approach was necessary.* A stepping back and trusting others to give him whatever consequences or accountability needed. Staying out of the way and stopping my enabling has been my toughest job.

> Doing the work to recover from enabling has reaped great benefits of stability in my life.

Some of our beloved family and friends with SUD are so entangled into the addiction behaviors, prison or the grave are the only options for them. When they have been kicked out of two rehabilitation centers, three or four sober living houses and two homeless shelters within three weeks, they are not manageable. Prison is better than the grave. Prison might be the only place where an active recovery plan may become desirable. I hope your circumstances are not this dire.

If sobriety is an issue, your loved one cannot succeed without addressing the root issues that are causing them to cope with substance use. You also may have substance use issues. It is difficult to correct another for their choices if you are making similar choices. This may be an opportune time to work a path together and hold each other accountable. Explore recovery options available in your area. If suicidal depression is noted, seek immediate professional counseling.

> My inner peace does not depend on someone else's sobriety.

There are great challenges in maintaining our emotional balance when loved ones are suffering with substance use disorders. This can be accomplished with stable boundaries, good support system, and a hefty dose of courage.

Sometimes, you cannot obtain your emotional balance until you have distanced yourself emotionally and physically from the one who is engaging in substance abuse without a desire to work an active recovery plan. If their recovery desire only comes when they are attempting to escape consequences, the consequences need to continue for the motivation for recovery to continue.

If you live with someone who grumps and causes you to have an emotional tailspin for half the day, you are too *emotionally dependent* upon this person. Perhaps, you have given them power over your heart. Current or past trauma could be making you vulnerable and extra sensitive and you may have *internal detachment* work to do to find your stability and healing.

INTERNAL DETACHMENT WORK

- Do not give anyone complete trust and access to your heart who has not earned it.
- If a person abuses your trust, take back your heart.
- Close your emotions to dysfunctional people.
- Do not give them the power to alter your mood.
- Do not give them the power to create internal or external chaos in your life.
- Avoid them. 1) Don't answer your phone or your door. 2) Don't look them in the face. 3)Don't let them engage you emotionally.

*Confrontation is not likely beneficial when dealing with an unstable person.

PRINCIPLE #3

Detachment is finding a healthy identity

My emotional stability is not dependent on another person or their sobriety.

SURVIVAL SKILLS WHEN LIVING WITH A PERSON WITH SUD

- Separate yourself emotionally and physically as much as possible.
- **Care less for the person with SUD's comfort and more for your own.**
- Build yourself up with healthy relationships. Understand that staying in toxic relationships means you will emotionally struggle.
- Enjoy your life. Talk less about their issues except occasionally with your closest friends.
- Join a support group and work *Enabler's Journey Recovery Plan*
- *Things usually become worse before they are better.* Understand if I interrupt recovery in a person with substance use disorder with enabling, they will likely relapse.
- Use outside authorities to hold them accountable.
- Understand the lower levels of love.
- Practice higher levels of love.

HIGHER AND LOWER LEVEL OF LOVE

Beloved means: one whom is greatly loved.

Developmental Stages of Love:

Lower levels of love

1. **Self-love** – empty, lonely, selfish, using others. Characterized by a life of confusion.
2. **False Love** – kind speech in words, but not in their heart. This type of love is very irritating.
3. **Enabling Love** – This person understands consequences and tries to remove the mountains in other people's lives. Usually these mountains are very important so the person can grow and mature and become strong. This person has faith, but their faith is usually in themselves or in money.
4. **Best Effort Love** – This person does a lot of charity work and gives of themselves. They do this to look good or to make up for other things that are not right. This type of love can be motivated by guilt or a need for approval and acceptance. Explore recovery in the area of "attachment disorders."

Higher levels of love (Understanding my life purpose)

5. **True Love** – Patient and Kind. This person wrestles their own stubborn self-will and pins it to the ground and pursues being a person that loves this way. **This person repents often.**
6. **Tough love** – This love is strong enough to allow others to have free will, make choices and suffer consequences. *This person trusts that others can find their own path.*
7. **Perfect Love** – Characterized by having <u>no fear</u>. Speak truth to yourself frequently and wrestle fear and pin it to the ground.
8. **Love your Higher Power and your neighbor as yourself**. This love

ENABLER'S JOURNEY DETACHMENT

is pure and seeks opportunity to help those in genuine need.

9. **Love with great peace** – This person will never take an offense. He will show compassion for the burdens of others. This person visits the sick, takes a meal to those with cancer or a new baby, etc. This person keeps their schedule loose enough to plan for the little interruptions in life.

10. **Everlasting love** – This love transcends time, space and all eternity and will love forever. This is a love that is more powerful than life. This is a place of safety and honor. When there is higher level of faithful, devoted, selfless, reciprocal love and devotion, you can be greatly loved and find someone you can safely love and become someone's beloved.

> Finding mature love means letting go of the lower levels of love. This will allow you to give and receive higher levels of love.

Healthy love does not fear letting go; sick love manipulates and controls consequences for irresponsible behavior which causes more dependency and prolongs suffering.

Think Effective Boundaries – At times, you may need to draw near your loved ones. At other times, you may need to move back from them to allow them space to work through the *developmental stages of love.*

- Have compassion and make a difference. Find good counselors, recovery centers, or support groups you and your loved one could attend. Lead the way and find recovery for yourself.

> Every individual with addictive behaviors has an enabler who is also sick. Individuals caught in addiction need more help than an enabler is capable of offering.

SELF-REFLECTION

Here are some great questions to work through with a trusted friend, support group or counselor.

- In what or whom is my identity? Is it in a higher power, my political influence, personal power or money? My career? My marriage or children?

- Do I think my loved one with SUD needs more money and their problems will be solved?

- Am I in constant anxiety?

- Could I use journaling to detach from my negative emotions?

- Do I refuse to be emotionally manipulated?

- Can I identify how I am being manipulated?

- Can I quiet my fears? What are my greatest fears?

- Do I think I have the power to change my loved one?

- Am I pulling my loved one out of the fire or am I being pulled in?

- Am I addicted to rescuing my loved one with addictive behaviors? Do I think rescuing is my responsibility?

- Am I gullible and believe everything I am told by my loved one with SUD?

- How could I investigate and hold people accountable?

- What am I doing that perpetuates the addictive cycle?

- How could I exercise my NO muscle?

- How can I make stronger boundaries if my boundaries aren't respected?

- How can I empower myself to become independent from abusers?

- Can I overcome cultural expectations and say no to an abusive parent, spouse or adult child?

- How long have I suffered abuse or neglect?

- Is this my first abusive relationship?

- Do I have any safe relationships?

- What have I done to attempt to resolve the issue?

- What could I do to change my circumstance? Outline your possible choices.

PRINCIPLE #4

Detachment respects the boundaries of others to make their own choices and to have their own consequences

BALANCE: STOPPING THE BITTERNESS

Bitterness comes when we are being over responsible, used or abused. Here are some things to do to stop your part of the addiction process.

- o No excuse making
- o No Interrupting consequences
- o Require accountability
- o Require them to work or pay their own fees/fines.
- o Stop making them comfortable

DEVELOPING BOUNDARIES

Developing healthy boundaries is foreign territory for most enablers. Here are some things to ponder.

- How can I say no with love and not hatred?

- How can I say NO without fear and anxiety?

- How can I respect another's choices when they say NO to recovery?

- What are my manipulative behaviors?

Write out what I will and will not tolerate?
I choose to not tolerate:

What am I able to tolerate without interrupting my own recovery from enabling and rescuing?

- What hinders me from following through with my choices?

- Have I built rigid and isolating walls that make me lonely? What can I do about this?

- Have I built strong boundaries that can be changeable and moveable if I choose to move them? In the past when I have changed a boundary, did it guide my loved one to achieve positive progression in recovery or was it used to deliver them from consequences and now their addiction patterns are stronger?

- If my boundaries aren't respected, I need stronger boundaries. What stronger boundaries could I implement to protect myself?

- How could I empower myself to be financially and emotionally independent enough to have my boundaries respected?

- How can I achieve personal growth? What do I need to work on most?

- How can I develop connectedness, and maturity with healthy individuals?

- Where is my focus? Is it on what I can't change or on what I can change?

- What worries consume me? Are they past, current or future worries?

    o Circle which worries written above are my responsibility.
    o Underline the ones that belong to someone else.
    o Place a box around the ones I can't do anything to amend; but, need to practice detachment.

Where and when do I need the most courage to face current circumstances?

Things to ponder:
- I can only control my decisions.
- I cannot control the final outcomes of those decisions.
- I am only responsible to change myself.
- I cannot manage another person's life choices.

PRINCIPLE #5

Detachment means minding my own business

If I am minding my own business, I will have the energy to address my issues and be positioned with others who can mentor, encourage and hold me accountable.

IDENTIFYING MY BEHAVIORS

- What unhealthy behaviors would I like to correct? (worry, fear, stress, anger, etc.)

- Can I refuse trauma/drama? Sometimes I create drama and cause myself unnecessary trauma. This keeps me in an emotionally heightened state. It would be equivalent to living my life on a roller coaster or in a war zone. Engaging in trauma/drama locks my body into a flight or fight response and gives me all the physical maladies of stress. This blocks me from being available emotionally to others. It places me in a react mode and not in a proactive mentality.

o How do I act when I lose my car keys?

o How do I respond to an inconvenience or interruption?

Take a day and evaluate how much stress you allow in your life. What would it look like if you didn't sweat the small stuff?

It is difficult to help anyone else if I am not good at confrontation. Keenly, I am aware of my ability to make a mountain out of ant hill. Sometimes, I can be over-focused on a minor issue because of a major situation I cannot change or control. The person I cannot safely confront can be making life-threatening decisions and my emotions can be so overwhelming that I shut down and over focus on little things.

o Can I work through my emotions before I confront someone?

Frequently, I pick at the safe people in my life, well, because they are safe. They won't hurt me or leave me. But this isn't fair to them. If I realize this, I can stop it. Then I can grieve for the loved one lost in addiction that I cannot save from his compulsions.

CONFRONTATION

Can I wait several days and work through my own emotions before I confront someone? Spend the time asking yourself some questions. Base your answers on your past experiences with this person and what you already know about their character.

- o What is my responsibility and what is not my responsibility?

- o Am I being petty?

- o Is this any of my business?

Before I give counsel to someone, I ask myself:
- o Do I have a strong relationship with this person?
- o Have I earned the right to be heard?
- o Are they asking for my counsel?

If not, I can back up and detach from their issue.

Sometimes if a person I love isn't asking for counsel, I **wait**. If I see something clearly in their life that is going to cause them trouble, I will ask them, "If I see something in your life that is out of balance would you want me to tell you?" This places them in a listening mode and makes me the coach or encourager. It also gives me permission to speak freely in love and respect their boundary if they say no. Then I can be quiet and not worry about it. Maybe they will be ready later and come back and ask for counsel.

This also validates them as a capable person who can make their own decisions. Then, I ask myself more questions. I can discern these answers based on my past experiences with this person.

o If I confront them, will they make me suffer more with their bullying, raging, or pouting?

o Will they make excuses or blame me?

o Will it be a productive conversation?

o Is this person emotionally stable enough to be confronted?

o Are my emotions under control or am I going to be the abuser?

o Will the results of the conversation likely add to my suffering?

o Am I passive/aggressive in my behaviors? This makes my environment unstable for me and my loved ones. *Passive/Aggressive is defined as ignoring an obvious problem until you explode from irritation or frustration.*

- o Is this person sober? Is he hungover? Is he in a drug seeking mode? *Drug seekers do a dance of rationalizing why they need their substance of choice. If you are attentive, you can identify a pattern of words or behaviors before a binge.*

Sometimes, I leech confrontation with passive/aggressive behaviors. There is a part of me that wants to be patient, but this good behavior of patience shouldn't make me a doormat to get run over. When it does, I become aggressive. Neither is good. There needs to be consistency in the way I behave. It takes energy to address issues on a consistent basis with empowering problem-solving skills.

- o Have I already confronted this person with the same issue many times before and I need to accept their decision or empower myself to move on?

- o What emotional baggage am I carrying that will interrupt my peaceful day? (Anger, sadness, fear, disgust, loneliness) Pick one and Journal about it here. Where do you feel the most helpless?

Now share this with a trusted friend or counselor.

Detachment is not about ignoring my emotions. It is about taking responsibility for myself and balancing my empathy for others. Then, I can detach from others who abuse or manipulate emotionally and financially. It can take a year of journaling and counseling to work through an issue to find emotional stability and to detach from people and circumstances I cannot change or control. If I get stuck in an exaggerated emotion for more than two weeks, I reach out for help from a trusted friend or counselor. *Exaggerated emotions are easy to identify because they are tormenting.* Knowing I am emotionally vulnerable to a certain person allows me to intentionally distance myself. This is needed for my protection. If a person can't hear me or ignores me, it is better to talk to a brick wall. I need to be quiet and detach emotionally to provide healthy space for myself.

MORE SELF EVALUATION

- Was there an event in childhood that caused me to become unbalanced?

- What is the most traumatic thing that has ever happened in my life? Have I resolved the emotional pain from this and detached it from my identity and formed a healthier identity?

- Is this my third or fourth unstable relationship? What part of my past do I keep repeating and trying to resolve?

- Do I believe it is my job to fix someone else? Do I consistently attract broken people and attempt to fix them? If so, my people-picker is broken.

Do I keep repeating my past?	
Do I choose friends based upon their appearance?	Do I look for deeper character qualities?
Do I have a constant need for approval and affirmation?	Can I give myself affirmation?
Do I trust too easily?	Can I withhold my trust until it is earned?
Do I move into relationships too quickly and then get scared and retreat?	Can I develop friendships slowly and learn to build trust with others without expectations?
Do I watch people and listen to how they talk about others?	Can I discern bitterness, anger or serious unresolved issues in the speech of another?
Is my relationship with my parent(s) poor?	Can I forgive and accept my family of origin?
Do I feel unloved?	Can I be kind to myself and work on my recovery journey?
Do I constantly feel lonely?	Can I reach out to safe and healthy support groups, hobby groups, book clubs, etc. and develop acquaintances without any expectations?

Can I identify areas of need in my life that may keep me choosing dysfunctional relationships?

HEALTHIER ME

- What negative mental thinking patterns need to change? Do I ruminate on negativity or can I control my thinking and enjoy my day? *Controlling my thinking is a developmental emotional skill.* This skill will be taught in the next recovery book on Emotional Maturity.

- What emotional response causes me the most suffering? (arguing, withdraw, isolation, etc.) What could I do differently?

- Physically what goals do I have to become physically healthy and fit?

- Financially what goals do I have to become secure in my future?

- What spiritual/emotional goals do I have for my life?

HEALTHY SPEECH EVALUATION

Rule: Kind, Patient and Firm	
1) Do I gossip?	
2) Do I nag?	
3) Do I complain?	
4) Do I slander others?	
5) Do I praise and affirm others?	
6) Do I consciously smile often?	
7) Do I think before I speak?	
8) Can I soften my tone and speak slowly?	
9) Am I patient with children and pets?	
10) Can I apologize for impulsive speech?	
11) Can I stop mid-sentence and take a breath and reword my response?	
12) Can kindness and patience be my rule, even when I need to be firm?	

BEHAVIOR EVALUATION

- Do I induce problems to manipulate or control others? Does someone else do this to control me?

- Do I harbor bitterness, resentments or un-forgiveness that leeches out on others and causes instability?

- Can I observe patterns of dysfunctional behaviors in others? For example: Does my loved one escalate an argument with me, so they have an excuse to abuse themselves with toxic substances and blame me?

- Do others create a new crisis every week or so to emotionally manipulate me financially? This is very common behavior for individuals with SUD or immature entitled adults.

- Can I recognize when others are lying to me?

- Am I compelled to offer help when others confide in me about their problems, even when they aren't asking for help? This is a hardcore rescuer/enabler.

- Can I give compassion without intervening when my loved ones are suffering from consequences of poor choices?

LIE IDENTIFICATION

- Assume if a person with active SUD is opening his mouth, he is lying.
- Verify everything before you believe anything.
- Do not be gullible.
- Make a recovering person with SUD earn your trust.
- Recognize your own lying habits or embellishments.

Habits are habits. Sometimes we learned to lie as children to avoid abuse. Other times, we were trained to lie by a manipulative parent. This will be a lifetime habit until we purpose to change it. I was thoroughly trained to lie for the purpose of manipulating people and circumstances. When I decided to break this habit, confessing constantly to a trusted friend was necessary. We agreed I was free to stop mid-sentence or to come back and correct my lying after the fact. This tactic was so humbling, that I quickly learned not to lie.

Developing trusting relationships means I need to be a trustworthy example for others to depend on and follow. As I become faithful in speaking the truth, I can require others to be accountable to earn my trust.

TRUST SCALE GUIDE

Never give a loved one with SUD a temptation:
• Never leave your purse out.
• Hide your wallet.
• Hide your identity: Social Security card/Birth Certificate
• Count your checks and keep them under lock and key (an active substance user will take a couple checks in the middle or back of the checkbook.)
• Never give passwords.
• Never give security codes.
• Never give house key.
• Never allow them to make a purchase with your debit/credit card.
• Never leave prescription medications unlocked.
• Never give them a key to the car. (Hide keys when not in use.)
• Lock your bedroom door at night if they are in the house.
• Get an alarm system.

Individuals in recovery need to earn trust: enablers and loved ones with SUD

PRACTICAL TIPS

Have I:
- made my bed?
- taken out my trash?
- cleaned up my yard?

If I **mind my own business,** I can have the energy to care for myself and address my character flaws and position myself with others who can mentor, encourage, and hold me accountable for my actions.

> A clear conscience brings a good night of sleep.

REFLECTIVE THINKING

- How can I practice quiet reflective thinking? Can I set a time of day or a special place to meditate and reflect on my day?

- Do I understand that often I cannot think my way through a problem, no matter how hard or how long I think about it? This is obsessive thinking, not quiet, productive thinking.

- Do I know how to meditate on wholesome thoughts?

- What can I do to quiet my fears?

- Do I know how to stay in the present moment and enjoy my day?

- Do I know how to detach from toxic people and circumstances I cannot control? This skill produces great peace.

- What consumes my passive thinking? Passive thinking are uninvited thoughts that take over quickly.

- How can I mature and develop a quiet mind?

- Do I know how to refuse a negative thought and replace it with a positive one?

- Do I recognize a toxic person who controls my thinking or emotions?

- What problems (from other people) would I need to release to find peace?

- What self-care priorities do I have in my daily routine?

- Do I need to say NO to others to better manage my time and prevent me from being overwhelmed?

- How could I tactfully do this?

- Is there a circumstance that has me paralyzed to make decisions?

- Can I be manipulated with urgency and factitious deadlines to make quick and foolish decisions? Do any recent examples come to mind?

- How does my addicted love one use other authorities to manipulate or extort from me financially? (The landlord, attorney, probation officer says this must be paid *now*.) This is commonly done on the day before you receive your paycheck. Watch for this cycle. Usually individuals with SUD squander their money and use your money for monthly expenses. Step back and let them learn.

- How can I prepare to change? Can I be slow to make decisions and involve other responsible people? Can I turn this over to someone else that cannot be manipulated emotionally?

- Who do I have in my life that would protect me from an abuser or manipulative person with SUD?

- What would I need to do to be compassionate and gracious to myself?

- Are there expectations I need to detach from? Are they mine or someone else's?

NEGATIVE EMOTIONAL TRIGGERS

- Which negative emotion(s) controls me?
  - Anger
  - Bitterness
  - Fear
  - Worry and Anxiety
  - Depression

If I am not an angry person, but compassionate and empathetic, it is necessary for me to use controlled anger to protect myself. Allowing myself to indulge some angry feelings can help me build a wall of protection around my heart to safeguard me from irresponsible adults.

- Journal to explore, release and change negative emotions. I journal beside a shredder. This way I am free to release all exaggerated emotions safely. If I keep the journal pages for a few days, I can reread them and laugh at how irrational I can be at times of stress. Writing forty ranting pages of what I cannot control brings out thoughts, emotions and lies I didn't know I believed. I journal until I can release the problem and unscramble my thinking and find peace. I start journaling with I hate... I am angry about... I am hurt about... I am disappointed about... I end my journaling with I forgive, I release, I am grateful for...

- How much time do I spend in negative rumination each day? Journal your negative thoughts, then attempt to change them to a positive thought. For example: I can't do anything right. Now change this to a positive statement. I can be patient with myself and do the best that I can do.

- Is my sleep interrupted by my worries? If so, lie upon your bed at night and visually put all your worries in a box and push them away. Then breathe deeply and clear your mind and focus on relaxing every part of your body. Start at your feet and work your way up. Let your breathing begin to deepen and lengthen.

- How much do I suffer for my loved one's immature decisions? Identify and write out all the things that are causing suffering. Now detach from this suffering by seeing the problem outside of you. It is not you, nor does it need to be inside of you. Move the emotional suffering to a safe distance from you. You may find your physical pain is associated with your emotional suffering. Breathe into your physical pain and visualize healing in that area. If you can detach from the emotional suffering, you will have energy to work a recovery plan to regain your physical, mental and emotional stamina.

- What if my suffering is from the death or imprisonment of a loved one? Detach from the loss of a dream or the sorrow of losing a loved one, then you can reshape your love for the person in a more realistic manner. If our loved one has died, we can comfort ourselves with memories of what we loved about them; and release any memory that causes suffering. We can reach out to a grieve recovery group.

- Can I mature and allow other adults to experience their own suffering? As a recovering enabler, we do not want to rescue our loved one from consequences, but we can have compassion and comfort them in their suffering. We can also guide them to let their suffering bring about lasting change in their lives for the better.

- Can I feel compassion without being responsible to act? If you relapse back into enabling when you see your loved one suffering, let someone else comfort them.

PERMISSION

- I give you permission to say NO.
- I give you permission to walk away from someone who only makes temporary changes to fool themselves and others.
- I give you permission to grieve and not be responsible for a loved one with SUD who refuses to work an active recovery plan with a sponsor and accountability.
- I give you permission to give a person with SUD or who is verbally abusive back their own problems. This is the loving thing to do for them and yourself.

UNMET NEEDS

When I have unmet needs, what negative behaviors do I exhibit?
- Mind altering substances (even prescription medications)
- Alcohol, excessive sugar, or overeating
- Sexually acting out
- Suicidal/homicidal/angry/bitter/self-pity/grieving rumination

- Compulsive shopping or gambling, television, etc.
    - o   What are my unmet needs?

    - o   Can I ask for what I need from safe people?

    - o   Do I know how to reach out to others?

    - o   Can I take care of my needs first? Enablers don't normally care for themselves.

    - o   Do I have a safe support group or close friends who understand?

    - o   If there is no one safe in my life, can I be safe for myself?

OBSESSIVE THINKING TRAPS

- **Fantasy thinking**
    - ▪   I compulsively escape the circumstances and reactions of others with fairytale daydreaming.

- **Trauma thinking**
  - I spontaneously and anxiously role play future devastation: bankruptcy, abandonment, homelessness, prison, and funerals.
  - Is he dead or in the gutter?
  - Is he at the bottom of the river?
  - What will happen to the children?
- **Automatic replay thinking**
  - I persistently replay a traumatic event, hurtful gesture or unkind word.
  - One harsh criticism gives me an avalanche of past wounds to rehearse. (This means I have not dealt with past trauma.)
  - I become paralyzed with self-pity type of behaviors. This can quickly overwhelm me with depression and isolation. It can be exhibited by overeating, staying in bed or addictive behaviors.

Self-pity zaps my strength.

It is vital to control our thinking. *Maturity can dictate what I will and will not think.* **Obsessive thinking can cause severe suffering and is addictive. It is a habitual pattern. Intentionally break it.**

Obsessive thinking causes confusion.

Reach out to a trusted friend, solid support group, and/or professional counselor to unravel this painful mess. If you do not, you will be driven to dysfunctional coping skills to alleviate your suffering. Undisciplined thinking will eventually take a toll on your physical health, well-being and all your other relationships.

BOUNDARIES WITH MY PASSIVE THINKING

Goals for my thinking:
1. Self-controlled
2. Healthy
3. Honorable
4. Faithful
5. Kind
6. Patient
7. Accepting
8. Releasing
9. True
10. Hopeful

When you hear thoughts that are robbing you of the enjoyment of your day, reject them and purposefully think wholesome thoughts. Give yourself ten minutes once or twice a day to think about problems and possible solutions. Set a timer. Keep a running list, spend those ten minutes worrying, fretting or being angry. When the timer goes off and you have found no viable solutions, get up and enjoy your day.

PRINCIPLE #6

Detachment means Forgiveness

Be kind and forgive.

Forgiveness can empower me to seek and search for ways to detach from my past and move forward with my life.

FORGIVENESS

If we don't forgive, we can't find forgiveness.

- Forgiveness should not allow someone else access to abuse us again.
- Forgiveness is free.
- **Trust is earned.**

If we indulge in unforgiveness, it will:

- Robs us of our happiness.
- Contaminate our thinking
- Contaminate our speech
- Cause troubles in our other relationships

HOW DO I FORGIVE

How do I forgive, when I don't feel like it?
1. Forgiveness is a choice and the right thing to do.
2. Forgiveness does not pardon the offender from consequences.
3. Forgiveness is for my benefit.
4. Forgiveness is not forgetfulness. It needs a strong boundary until trust is earned.

BITTERNESS

Unforgiveness will end in bitterness that will ooze a little at a time or explode in exaggeration over trivial matters. If you leech bitter poison onto waitresses or retail workers, become cognizant of the unsafe person in your life that you cannot confront. Journal or find a trusted friend and unload the pain in a healthy manner. This will help you detach your heart from an unsafe person who may never acknowledge their wrong or ask for forgiveness.

- Bitterness robs our joy for today.
- Bitterness clouds our memories of yesterday.
- Bitterness overshadows every future relationship with lonely walls of self-protection.

Truth

- If we do not forgive, we will be the one who is tormented.
- Un-forgiveness holds us hostage in hatred, anger and suffering.
- Forgiveness does not mean forgetfulness.
- Forgiveness should not open us up to an unsafe relationship.

- If we accept the suffering caused by another and forgive our offender this releases us.
  - Forgiveness brings us emotional stability and tranquility.
  - Forgiveness softens our hearts to become responsible for our part of the problem.
  - Forgiveness forges the way for others to humbly repent.
  - Repentance is a fresh, clean slate.
  - Repentance is permission to move forward, learn, grow and **not repeat the past.**

Forgiveness is separate from reconciliation.

RECONCILIATION

- Reconciliation comes when the other person acknowledges their dysfunctional behaviors and develops a plan to change with structured accountability.
- Reconciliation, if pursued too quickly, may cause your loved one to fall back into old habits of dominance and manipulation. It may also allow you to be abused again.

REPENTANCE

Repentance for our enabling behaviors is part of our recovery. Repentance reminds us that enabling is sick love and is not helping others find maturity, stability, or independence.

ENABLING

1. Enabling keeps others dependent upon me.
2. Enabling causes toxic and unhealthy relationships.
3. Enabling relieves my suffering temporarily; but, causes more grief and anguish long term.
4. Enabling cripples my loved ones from being responsible.
5. Enabling has the opposite effect than what I intended.
6. Enabling causes confusion in all my other relationships.
7. Enabling distances my healthy family and friends.
8. Enabling results in more guilt, shame and despair.

I am responsible to stop my enabling!

I am not responsible for an irresponsible adult person's financial needs. For example: Bail money, fees, fines, car payments, gas, insurance, child support, housing, food, clothing, health care, etc.

Enabling destroys the potential for a healthy identity.

HOLIDAYS

Enabling makes for uncomfortable holidays. If my loved one isn't in active recovery, he shouldn't be allowed to bring his manipulative games and confusion to holiday family gatherings. And I shouldn't guilt others into accepting this nonsense into their homes and around their children, just to keep up the appearance of a normal family. A person with SUD is the one responsible for earning the trust of siblings, step-parents, or extended family members by making restitution for past wrongs and working a strong recovery program. A truly recovering person with SUD will make his own path back to his family. Any coercion from me places the whole family in danger.

Yes, danger! If I stop enabling my loved one, he will seek out other victims to enable him.

- **I do not want to leave a legacy of being a doormat.**
- **I do not want my children and grandchildren to think it is noble to find toxic people and attempt to rescue them.**
- **I want to empower them and give them permission to develop mutually loving and healthy families of their own.**

SUFFERING

- Realize suffering is a part of this world.
- Let your suffering make your heart a tender protector of innocent children.
- Do not be tender towards the adults pretending to be victims to escape the consequences of their poor choices.
- **Let suffering do the teaching.** Suffering helps us all make choices to change. Then, our future can look different from our past.

List the good things that have come from the experience of your greatest suffering.

List what you will and will not do again.

Now, develop future relationship goals. Where do you want to be in a month, a year, and in five years?

RELATIONSHIP GOALS

What are the characteristics of my dream relationship?

Is this realistic or fairytale thinking?

What are the characteristics of your current close relationships? Name each person and place one main word beside their name which would describe them.

Which relationships above are safe and secure?

Which ones are semi-safe?

Which ones are painful and unstable?

Which ones are toxic and drive you crazy?

Take one relationship and make goals:
One year:

Two years:

Five years:

Age 60 and beyond: Where would you like to be in your relationships when you may need assistance or compassion? Seniors are more vulnerable to lying, irresponsible cons and embezzlers.

What would you have to do now to meet these future goals?

What would your loved one need to do? Are they willing or able to work on the relationship to make themselves dependable and safe?

What relationships do you need to nurture the most? Think of trustworthy, dependable, hard-working, protective, or innocent when you make this choice.

What relationships do you need to distance yourself from? Consider distance with people who are unpredictable, angry, lying, manipulative or abusive. Guard your heart and expect less from people who are emotionally unavailable.

What relationships have you invested in for 5-10 years?

Are the people you invest in growing healthier or unhealthier every year?

How has this affected you?

If there is no current potential for growth, is this a relationship you want to continue investing in?

POWER TO STOP THE ENABLING

Healing comes when we obtain beneficial counseling and stop the enabling cycle.

- Only I have the power to stop the agony of enabling in my life.
- Detach from the past.
- Move forward.
- Stop dragging others to recovery who refuse to change.
- If others want to change, they will follow you into healthy counseling and accountability.
- If they don't want to change, *step over them* and move towards a healthier you. This is healthy!

- **Stop looking back!** We can't change or fix someone who is hell-bent on reckless destruction.
- The behavior of taking responsibility for your own growth may inspire others to do the same.
- Make little decisions to build your confidence.
- What little decisions could you make today?

PRINCIPLE #7

Detachment means thinking differently

I can identify the thoughts I think about myself. Whose voice is in my head rejecting or controlling me?

SELF TALK

What do you think about yourself?

Is there a voice rejecting you?

Has someone stolen your identity? How confident are you in yourself?

Find a refuge. A quiet place to claim what is yours with kindness and firmness.

The individual with SUD's battle does not belong to me.
I cannot win sobriety for my loved one.

My *victory* is secured by exercising my right to say NO with firmness and kindness. Analyze your beliefs. If you believe any of the lies below, you have lost your identity and the right to enjoy your life.

Analyze the should and shouldn't lies in your belief system.

I should always help my family	I shouldn't let them suffer.
I should never turn my back on a dysfunctional parent or adult child.	I shouldn't abandon self-destructive people.
I should keep picking up after irresponsible adults.	I shouldn't expect them to respect my boundaries.
I should keep the peace and be passive at all cost.	I should apologize if I offend them.
I shouldn't say NO.	I shouldn't bring up the past.
I should keep bailing them out. Prison is too harsh.	I shouldn't confront poor behaviors.
I should sacrifice my life for theirs.	I shouldn't fight back.
I should put their needs above my own.	I shouldn't expect them to be able to change.

Courage is the secret to overcoming enabling behaviors.

PRINCIPLE #8

Detachment means if I see a tornado
coming, I can hide in the cellar.

I can find ways to disentangle co-dependent, enabling behaviors. I can detach from people who systematically control and manipulate me to finance their irresponsible behaviors. I can withdraw from those who are disorderly and understand it is not my responsibility to feed or house able bodied adults who refuse to work or squander resources.

RULES FOR SURVIVAL

- If a man doesn't work, he shouldn't eat.
- Make no friendship with stupidity.
- Withdraw yourself from confusion and disorder.
- **Have nothing to do with an angry person.** Do not engage them until they have control over their emotions. **Walk away!**
- **Most likely you have warned them a hundred times. They aren't listening.**
- Warn a person once, warn them twice and then have nothing to do with him until they develop a viable accountability plan to change.

| My sanity is too important to indulge immature emotions and behaviors.

What boundaries do you need to set up in your life?

What boundaries are being violated?

What can you do to empower yourself to be able to control your own environment and make it safer for you or your children?

What children need to be protected?

What could you do about this? Is there something another parent or loved one is trying to do that you might emotionally support and empower to care for the children?

PRINCIPLE #9

*Detachment means to bear another
person's crisis, but to let him carry his
own personal load*

A crisis is an accident, injury, severe illness, or natural disaster. A personal load is paying my own utilities, car insurance, car payments, gas and food. I am not talking about the fiscally responsible working poor, ill or sober homeless.

CRISIS

- Accident, tragedy, natural disaster, severe illness or a major loss.

PERSONAL LOAD

- Let others climb their own mountains. This develops their strength.
- Let them be responsible to pay their utilities, car insurance, car payment, gas or food.

  We are considering one who has squandered their provisions on cigarettes, movies, drugs, alcohol, gambling, or frivolous shopping and eating out. We are not talking about the responsible working poor, or ill.

- In this case, you may want to take your loved one to a financial course and teach them to manage their money.
- Help them understand how to live within their financial means.
- You may want to help empower them to achieve more employable job skills.
- Public transportation assistance may be needed for a month or so during early recovery phase.
- Independence is an important step for confidence.
- Assistance is only for one in active recovery.

ENTANGLEMENT GAUGE

Evaluate yourself and how entangled you are with an irresponsible adult or active substance user and how much of their personal load you are carrying for them:	
1. Providing Food	
Taking them out to eat frequently (or cooking for them)	
2. Providing Transportation	
3. Gas card	
4. Credit card	
5. Car insurance	
6. Health insurance	
7. Paying car payment or buying a car for a person with a history of DUI's	
8. Free (on demand) childcare	
9. Providing housing	
10. Paying rent or buying them a home	

11. Letting individual with substance use disorder live with you	
12. Picking up after them	
13. Doing their laundry	
14. Paying utilities	
15. Paying routine bills, cellphones, cable, internet, etc.	
16. Buying nice clothes	
17. Paying for haircuts	
18. Making excuses for them	
19. Co-signing for them	
20. Paying fees, fines, and other legal expenses	
21. Giving them false references for jobs	
22. Cashing checks for them or writing checks without reimbursement	
23. Paying unexpected bills: car repairs, doctor bills, prescriptions, etc.	
24. Paying for bad checks.	
25. Hiring attorneys to get them out of trouble.	
26. Berating, bullying, shaming, or manipulating other family members to enlist help for the loved one with SUD.	

This scale will help you identify how deeply you are entangled with an irresponsible adult. Enablers with a "stand them up" and "fix them up" philosophy make their loved one appear to be responsible. This sets up the person with SUD to prey on unsuspecting victims. These victims could be left beaten, pregnant and with their credit ruined within 4-6 months. It also sets up the person with SUD to acquire jobs where they can abuse other employees and rob employers.

ACTIVE RECOVERY

- Recovering loved one's with SUD allow family and friends to question them and hold them accountable for time, money, friends, activities, etc.
- They are, also, actively pursuing an accountability group and individual sponsorship through a support group.

> Support is a road to somewhere, not a road to nowhere.

- The basement or the couch is nowhere.
- It is important to let them learn quick and early to carry their own personal load or their financial struggles will snowball.

If I become a pushover for the irresponsible, I will reap the consequences. If I am over-responsible, it will allow others to be under-responsible.

Here is a list of true recovery behaviors. This list will help you understand if you are being deceived. It will help your loved one in addiction understand if he is deceiving himself. *Most loved one's with SUD have no clue the work that needs to be done to achieve the future they desire.*

TRUE AND FALSE RECOVERY

Unless you can identify the difference between true and false recovery, it is impossible to know if your loved one is beginning to recover. As you recover from enabling and your loved one begins recovery, strong boundaries and distance in the relationship are most likely necessary.

True Recovery	False Recovery
Broken heart… grieving over their losses	Sorry for consequences, not poor behaviors
Paying back anything stolen	Lots of emotions, crying, anger, mood swings
Setting boundaries to prevent themselves from falling back into old habits	Good behavior (temporarily) to make up for wrongs
Setting up accountability partners	Self-destructive thinking/behaviors
Being open and accountable in every area of life	Saying "I am sorry." No plan to change.
Confessing past wrongs (with trusted person) Developing a plan for restitution.	Makes excuses (hiding full truth/blaming others)
Seeking help	Trying to weasel out of consequences
Sticking to a plan developed by counselor/authority	Refusing to talk over issues. "No one tells me what to do." *Demands blind trust.*
Walking daily in recovery.	Playing a good game, while they are learning to become a functional alcoholic or substance user.

PRINCIPLE #10

Detachment means to allow myself to
learn from my mistakes

This does not mean I will brood, beat myself up or turn to destructive behaviors. It is an honest evaluation of my actions and their outcomes. Then, I can pursue a plan to make my future look different from my past.

BROKENNESS

- Brokenness over past mistakes is not wailing and wallowing in despair.
- It is not brooding or beating myself up.
- It is not self-destructive behaviors.

Brokenness is a death of my expectations.

- A coming to an end of myself and releasing all my wishes and desires, then detaching from what I cannot control.
- It is an acceptance of the inability to change others.

BOUNDARIES

- Nothing is free. Charge recovering adults for food, bedroom space, basement space, utilities, childcare, etc. Expect them to help financially.
- You may save the money you charge them for a down payment on rent or a car if progressive recovery is viable.
- All assistance is based upon recovery.
- Stealing is not tolerated.
- Drug or alcohol use of any kind is not tolerated in your home.
- House rules need to be established and followed.
- Young adults with serious substance use issues are not allowed to stay in your home to learn to become functional substance users.
- Whining and belly aching is not to be tolerated.

Kindness and respect is a boundary not to be crossed.

FUNCTIONAL ADDICTIONS

- Individuals with functional addictions can function in society while denying there is a problem. Save yourself a lot of suffering and let them function somewhere else.
- A well-structured sober living house on a bus route may be a good option.

SEVERE ADDICTIONS

Severe addictions make individuals dysfunctional; they push through every boundary. If you give them an inch, they take a mile. They play the charmer and take every advantage to manipulate, coerce and dominate with a smile. Anyone who tells them NO or attempts to protect someone from their manipulation is immediately attacked and made into the villain. The person with severe addiction is a master at playing the victim. He can also become suicidal, homicidal or violent at any time. You cannot help this person if they will not take personal responsibility for their actions! They need accountability and more boundaries than an enabler could ever give them. If they are out of control and overdosing, they need confinement through legal means they cannot manipulate.

| Enablers need to detach and get out of the way.

One person with SUD you may be able to help. Another one no one can help; they must want their recovery enough to fight for it. Many recovering from addiction have too much anxiety to function in society and maintain sobriety. Find a long-term rehabilitation center that has a program to reintegrate them back into society. Employment at a rehabilitation facility as a cook or grounds keeper may give them stability. It will consistently remind them of the suffering of life consequences of addiction as they see it played out in the lives of others. Another viable option would be a sober living home with accountability, sponsorships and group meetings.

Detaching from a toxic person is your recovery goal. It is maturing and healing and trusting others to find their own way in life. It is vital for the safety of the elderly, abused and innocent children.

Total abandonment of a loved one with SUD is devastating. This is never optimal. Only you can discern if the substance use, patterns of abuse, neglect of duty, abandonment of responsibility, chronically blaming others and refusal of personal responsibility is toxic.

If our loved one with SUD becomes aggressive, defensive or violent when confronted, they are not safe. They leave you no choice. If they are going to drown you, self-preservation must be priority. Enablers would die for their loved ones if it would help. Where does it stop?

Even if we give them everything, the chaos won't stop. An active substance user is no longer in control of their decisions. When they are driven by addictions, they have allowed themselves to be devoured and become a devourer. This bear is not tamable by any enabler, no matter how much of ourselves we sacrifice.

Functional Addiction	Severe Addiction

Schooling
• Struggling
• May need trade school or apprenticeship
• Short term goals
Rehabilitation
  • Denial of problem
  • Avoidance of issues
	Schooling
	• Drop out
	• Irresponsible
	• Undisciplined
	Rehabilitation
	• Leave rehab center
	• Return and leave again and again

Employment • Calls off work often • Health issues • Struggles with relationships • Struggles to submit to authority	Employment • Quit • Fired • Blames others • Complains • Won't submit to authority
Relationships • Mostly verbal abuse • Sometimes extreme ranting • Intoxicated or high when not at	Relationships • Violent/abusive/raging • Easily provoked • Abandons responsibilities

work	• Domestic violence
• Divorced or unstable relationships	• Child abuse or neglect
• Trouble managing finances	• Entitled behaviors
Courts	**Court accountability**
• Pays own fines	• House arrest
• Learns temporarily from consequences	• Imprisonment
	• Probation
	• Forced Counseling
	• Forced Rehabilitation
	• Sober Living home
Character	**Character**
• Insecure	• Lies, cheats, steals
• Poor coping skills	• Deceptive, manipulative
• A good heart	• Selfish
Our Boundaries	**Our Boundaries**
• Move in and out of this relationship	• Boundaries usually won't be respected
• Let them know calls will be blocked for one week if they call intoxicated	• Boundaries will be manipulated.
• Let them know they will not be invited to family functions for one year if they show up intoxicated.	• Most likely distance will be needed until progressive recovery is pursued.
• Give them back their problems	• This person will only seek recovery when forced to do so.
• Set boundaries with obsessive ranting, hang up or walk away.	• Turn over to court authorities
• Encourage counseling	• Do not enable destructive behaviors
	• Be careful to not confront them

• Support groups • Sponsors	alone • Understand this is an unsafe relationship
Outcomes: • Depends upon loved ones developing healthy strong boundaries • Depends upon healthy confrontation and accountability	Outcomes: • Unstable • Unpredictable • Chaos • Confusion • Life threatening overdoses • Health issues • Homelessness
My response: • Forgive quickly • Refuse to be in relationship with them if they are under the influence • Refuse exaggerated, immature emotions • Frequently reach out to them • Send notes and cards of encouragement	My response: • Protect the elderly and the children • Distance and detachment • Allow them to have their choices and their own consequences • Grieve and detach • Hope for the best • Leave their future in their hands

You cannot help a person if they will not take personal responsibility for their actions!

PRINCIPLE #11

Detachment means emotionally separating myself from the problem.

This is simple, but not easy. Immaturity soaks up the emotions around me and mirrors them back. As I mature emotionally, I can feel my own emotions and let others feel their own. I can change the things I can and release the things I cannot change and purpose to enjoy my day.

EMOTIONAL SEPARATION

- This is easy, but not simple. Do I have my own identity? Or is my identity wrapped up in another?

- Immaturity soaks up the emotions of others around us and mirrors them back. If another is angry, can I refuse to be angry in response?

- Can I distinguish between my emotions and the emotions of others?

- Am I controlled emotionally? Do others manipulate my decisions with tears, anger, depression?

- Am I too empathetic? Do I rescue others from consequences of their poor choices?

- How could I harden my heart against smiling embezzlers and coercive manipulators? This is not cold; it is honorable self-preservation.

Ruling my own emotions is shutting out the nonsense around me.

- Maturity recognizes the emotion and feels it intensely and then releases it quickly.
    - This takes quieting myself to reflect on my day with mature observational skills and observing my emotions. Study your emotions and identify when and why they change.
    - This takes allowing myself space to meditate and reflect.
    - Maturity practices releasing the negative emotions that cause me suffering.

For lasting recovery, an enabler must see straight through the pretense of an individual with Substance Use Disorder.

> Ruling my own emotions is the key to enjoying my day.

Name the emotionally manipulative, people, places or circumstances you need to avoid.

HEALTHY SEPARATION

- Healthy separation is a refusing to think on, act on, or be involved in things that are none of my business. What things am I entangled in that are none of my business?

There is a healthy separation from adult children. A launching them into independent living to care for themselves and solve their own problems.

- I may listen, counsel and give advice.
- I may give warnings of potential pitfalls ahead if they continue the path they are on.
- I may do research and help them look at options.
- I must see their problems as theirs, not mine. I am not their fixer upper.
- I may make deadlines and gradually add more boundaries

and give the adult recovering from SUD more responsibilities.

- I may not manipulate with emotions, money or approval.
- Withdrawal of support will follow irresponsible choices. That's not manipulation. It is consequences to their choices.
- I may tell them that I trust them to find their own path in life. I am on their side. I know they can do it.

ACTIONS IN RESPONSE TO DANGEROUS BEHAVIORS

- I will call probation officers if lying, stealing, or substance use returns.
- I will arrange for an arrest if I know they are driving while intoxicated.
- I will give them addresses to homeless shelters if they are disrespectful to me and live in my home.
- I will call the police and place a protective order against them if they threaten me.
- I will not allow them to drive my car if they are irresponsible with their choices.
- I will call protective services if I know of child abuse or neglect.
- If they have money to eat out, buy cigarettes and movies, they have money for their bills.
- I *will not* loan them money, if previous loans are unpaid.
- I *will not* bail them out of jail.
- I *will not* pay for an attorney.

Coddling leads to a life of suffering and dependency.

| We must develop tough love and stop being part of the problem.

BOUNDARIES TO CONSIDER WITH THOSE IN ACTIVE SUD

1) Abusive calls will result in being blocked for one week.
2) Thefts or manipulation will result in one month of no contact.
3) Intoxication or being high around me or the children will result in 6 month-one year of no contact.
4) Threats of violence will result in a protective order.

What consequences will you give your loved one who violates your boundaries?

Your boundaries can only be enforced by you. If you are not in a place of safety, work on safety and stability first. If you are not in a place of power, work on empowering yourself to achieve financial independence.

Sometimes our lives are so chaotic there are no good options. All our options seem distasteful.

What are your options? Line out even the distasteful ones. It may take looking at your situation from all sides to find viable change.

PRINCIPLE #12

Detachment means I can enjoy my day.

Detachment is not abandonment, but a healthy love for me and others. I can make decisions without fear or emotional manipulation. This includes gradual separation and launching of adult children into independent living. If I coddle adult children, it is more likely they will have a life of suffering and co-dependency.

DETACHMENT IS LOVE

Detachment is making decisions based upon long terms goals. It is done without emotions. It is a conscience choice to enjoy the day.

UNHEALTHY WAYS OF CARING

- Rescuing
- Coercing
- Manipulating
- Taking charge of dysfunctional adults
- Paying their bills

- Making excuses
- Overreacting
- Under reacting
- Walking on eggshells
- Demanding
- Controlling

HEALTHY WAYS OF CARING

- Choosing what is best for me.
- Boundaries against the immature or abusive.
- Holding others accountable for thefts.
- Calling them out on their lies.
- Giving our loved one direction on where to receive help.
- Leaving the decision for recovery in the hand of the one with SUD.
- Distancing myself from anyone with active addictive behaviors.
- *Protecting my heart by loving them with my head and not my emotions.*

The greatest detachment skill to learn is to die to emotions.

If I am dead (detached) to my emotions, I cannot be manipulated emotionally. I can make decisions that are rational, planned, thought out and purposeful.

Do not be an emotional puppet or an easy target for the financial extortion of a person with addictive behaviors.

All addiction behaviors whether they are drugs, alcohol, gambling, food, workaholics, enabling, television, games or any other self-indulgent comforting is rooted in an emotional wound and/or unmet needs. Recovery explores these issues deep within our souls and helps us develop a plan for lasting change.

| All addictive behaviors are destructive and cause suffering.

HEART EVALUATION

- A **calloused heart** is stuck in pain, refuses change, and stays in a vicious, sick cycle.
- A **surrendered heart** is totally releasing others, working on myself and producing a "Free Spirit".
- An **emancipated heart** is free to enjoy my life, no matter what!!!

| Enabling is emotional slavery to a loved one with SUD.

Learn to find the good in great times of sorrow.
When destructive behavior patterns cannot be broken:
- Stop
- Acknowledge negative thinking
- Surrender what cannot be changed
- Practice quietness inside and pursue contentment
- *Contentment* is an emotional **developmental skill of maturity** which must be intentionally cultivated.
- This inner peace can give you the strength to change your life.

COUNT THE COST

If you have done this detachment work, the grieving will stop, and you will be able to enjoy your life. If you are still lacking your own identity you might coddle and enable a child to become irresponsible to attempt to find your completeness in yet another person. Also, as you release dysfunctional relationships, you may inadvertently shift your attention onto a semi-healthy relationship and start trying to manipulate a different person.

Think about a functional relationship you are focusing on and ask yourself some questions:

1) How much do you walk on eggshells?

2) How often is communication stifled with eye rolling, sighing, grumping or growling?

3) How much anger or bullying do you tolerate?

4) How much do you fear this person?

5) How much do you enjoy this person?

6) How much shared power is there in the relationship?

7) Are your emotional needs being met?

8) How much do your cry or grieve for the person you know they could be?

9) Compared to five years ago has this person become stronger and closer to you or have they withdrawn and regressed emotionally?

10) How long have you tried to repair this person: physically, mentally, emotionally, socially or financially?

11) Do you feel safe, cared for, protected or cherished?

12) What cost are you willing to pay to continue this relationship?

13) How often does this person pout, sulk, or become moody and broody if you confront them?

14) How much work are you doing in this relationship?

15) Is this person emotionally available to you? Are they approachable?

16) Is this a healthy, trusting, transparent relationship?

When your needs are consistently ignored, or you are controlled, blamed or violated, anger and bitterness are common. Anger is safer than grieving the loss of the hopes and dreams of this relationship. Yet you cannot live a healthy life grieving year after year. Living with a chronic irritation or chronically being irritated is draining. So, what are you to do?

Take back portions of your heart. A hardened heart makes life bitter. A walled heart with windows and doors makes life protected and safe for others to come and go. Use your windows to determine the level of safety. Use your doors to invite others in and to shut out unsafe people. Use your walls to give yourself protection and safe place to develop your own inner strength and personal stability.

If your functional loved one doesn't feel the need to be connected and it is not in your best interest to leave, built a wall around your heart. To stay or leave is not the question. *The question is can you accept this person the way they are without manipulating, fretting or grieving and enjoy your life to the fullest with or without their participation.* Give the people in your life freedom to find their own path. The goal is a healthy vibrant life for you. Stop your grieving. Accept what is not within your power to change and follow your own hopes and dreams.

FINAL THOUGHTS

Remain conscience of your detachment work, or you may detach from everyone and everything and be emotionally numb. This feels empty, isolating and vulnerable. Dysfunctional detachment can be a survival skill learned because of unprocessed abuse and trauma and an unsafe environment. It can end in pseudo attachments to destructive people and behaviors like substance abuse to fill the emptiness. We often see this in teenagers who give their allegiance to rebellious friends or destructive habits. They also may engage in high risk behaviors and become thrill seekers to attempt to feel again.

Today I want you to consciously detach from the places, people, emotions, circumstances and traumas of the present and the past. Then I want you to intentionally attach to safe people, safe place, safe memories and realistic future hopes and dreams. Safe people are safe to love. They will disappoint and let you down, but you will be safe to return to them and work out relationship problems without blame and anger.

Enablers can have normal relationships that cause them suffering because of their over focus on managing the attitudes and behaviors of others. If your functional relationships continue to make you suffer, explore your expectations and work on acceptance.

Detachment is A Developmental Emotional Maturity Skill needed to survive in a relationship with a person with Substance Use Disorder. Detachment is needed to recover from past abuse and traumas. Detachment takes courage. Detachment means not being controlled by emotions, but determining needed actions based upon logical reasoning. It is not passive, but purposeful. Detachment is stopping the chaos and confusion. Detaching from the vile leaves room for the precious.

| Detach from the vile and attach to the precious!

EMOTIONAL MATURITY SKILL REVIEW

Emotional maturity isn't accidentally developed. Here are some of the developmental emotional maturity skills we have touched on in this book.

1) Don't take abusive words as truth or internalize them.
2) Separate your identity from irrational thinking.
3) Learn your life lessons
4) Be aware of false thinking patterns.
5) Purposefully develop higher levels of love
6) Deal with your exaggerated emotions.
7) Control your thinking
8) Detach from toxic people and circumstances
9) Contentment

For more study and insight into these concepts and many other developmental emotional skills work through our upcoming book called *Developmental Emotional Maturity Skills: Enabler's Journey Recovery Series Book Three*. In this book you will learn to identify and recognize emotions as information and detach from them to stop suffering and develop your own identity.

May you find healing.
May you find rest and peace.
May you find hope in your recovery.
May you trust your loved one to find his own path in life.
May you find courage to reclaim yourself and enjoy your day.
--Angie, Perry and Sarah

DETACHMENT QUICK GUIDE

Healthy love does not fear letting go; sick love manipulates and controls consequences for irresponsible behavior which causes more dependency and prolongs suffering.

#1 Detachment is not cold, withdrawn or isolated, but a decision to do what is best for myself first. It is a healthy boundary of knowing where my responsibility begins and where it ends. It is a healthy separation from toxic relationships and a healthy connectedness with others.

#2 Detachment is not caring less but caring more for my emotional stability. In this step, I need to understand my level of enmeshment. *Enmeshment is being entangled or wrapped up in someone else so much that I have lost my identity and have no peace.*

#3 Detachment is understanding my emotional stability is not dependent on another person or their sobriety.

#4 Detachment respects the boundaries of others to make their own choices and to have their own consequences.

#5 Detachment means "minding my own business". I will then have the energy to address my issues and be positioned with others who can mentor, encourage and hold me accountable.

#6 Detachment means forgiveness. This can empower me to seek and search for ways to detach and "let go" of my past and move forward with my life.

#7 Detachment means thinking differently. I can identify the thoughts I think about myself. Whose voice is in my head rejecting or controlling me?

#8 Detachment means if I see a tornado coming, I can hide in the cellar. I can find ways to disentangle my codependent, enabling behaviors. I can detach from people who systematically control and manipulate me to finance their irresponsible behaviors. I can withdraw from those who are disorderly and understand it is not my responsibility to feed able bodied adults who refuse to work or squander resources.

#9 Detachment means to help bear another person's crisis, but to let him carry his own personal load. A crisis is an accident, injury, severe illness, or natural disaster. A personal load is paying my own utilities, car insurance, car payments, gas and food. I am not talking about the fiscally responsible poor, ill or sober homeless.

#10 Detachment means to allow myself to learn from my mistakes. This does not mean I will brood, beat myself up or turn to destructive behaviors. It is an honest evaluation of my actions and their outcomes. Then, I can pursue a plan to make my future look different from my past.

#11 Detachment means emotionally separating myself from my problem. This is simple, but not easy. Immaturity soaks up the emotions around me and mirrors them back. As I mature emotionally, I can feel my own emotions. I can change the things I can and release the things I cannot change and purpose to enjoy my day.

#12 Detachment means I can let go of another person's problem, choose to let them mature, and become stronger by allowing them to find their own solutions. Detachment is not abandonment, but a healthy love for me and others. I can make decisions without fear or emotional manipulation. This includes gradual separation and launching of adult children into independent living. If I coddle adult children, it is more likely they will have a life of suffering and dependency.

The decisions I make will be rational, thought out and purposeful. I will not be an emotional puppet or a soft target for an addicted extortionist. I can guard myself from abuse with strong boundaries. I will acknowledge my

ENABLER'S JOURNEY DETACHMENT

addictive behaviors and dysfunctional coping skills, including my behavior of rescuing and enabling. I will search for the root of my problems: a past wound, unmet need, guilt, a desire to keep my loved one from experiencing pain, or public embarrassment. Perhaps it is the misery of the consequences of defective choices, which will propel my loved one into recovery. In recovery, we can both encounter others to encourage, support us and find lasting peace. *The spiraling financial consequences, mental anguish, emotional chaos, and physical drain of enabling begs the voice of detachment to ensure self-preservation precisely as an Artic Expeditioner would strategically plans for his survival.*

AUTHOR'S BIOGRAPHIES

Angie G. Meadows graduated from St Mary's School of Nursing as a Registered Nurse, Marshall University with a Bachelor's in Nursing and Ohio State University with a Master's in Nursing. She has worked at multiple hospitals in multiple capacities. Angie has been a keen observing of human behaviors as she has dealt with enablers and those with SUD over the years. She is currently a wife, mother, speaker and writer. Her favorite past time is quilting.

Dr Perry Meadows graduated from Marshall University with a Bachelor of Science in chemistry, Master of Science in Biological Sciences, and Doctor of Medicine. Dr. Meadows completed his internship and residency at Marshall University School of Medicine in Family Practice and is a Fellow of the American Academy of Family Physicians. Dr. Meadows also received his Juris Doctor from Salmon P. Chase College of Law, Northern Kentucky University and M.B.A. from Regis University. Dr. Meadows speaks on a local, regional, and national level on topics related to substance use disorder. He is active in working with various community organizations across Central Pennsylvania in issues related to behavioral health and substance use disorder.

Sarah J Meadows graduated from Liberty University with a bachelor's degree in psychology. She has worked in the public-school system as a Therapeutic Day Treatment Counselor. She is currently pursuing a master's degree in Clinical Mental Health Counseling. Sarah enjoys her friends and her beloved corgi.

OTHER RESOURCES BY THE AUTHORS

A Thousand Tears: An Enabler's Journey **ISBN: 9781732810204**

This 240+ pages, 24 chapters to identify the Enabler Cycle and our conflict with individuals in addiction. We will also be able to identify a manipulator, devourer or toxic relationship in our life and learn to confront and detach. This book is a useful tool in dealing with individuals with Substance Use Disorder or irresponsible behaviors. It also includes multiple self-assessment tools: Enabler's paradigm, entanglement gauge, anxiety quotient, trust scales, and much more. This is the original Enabler's Journey work and is a condensed version of all the smaller books in the Enabler's Journey Series.

An Enabler's Journey: A Christian Perspective **ISBN: 9781732810211**

This book is 290+ pages and 24 chapters. It is almost the same book as *A Thousand Tears: An Enabler's Journey* except it has more than a 100 Scriptures to validate the principles for dealing with people in relationships.

Enabler's Journey Recovery Plan: Enabler's Journey Recovery Series: Book 1 **ISBN: 9781732810228** This is a 100+ pages Book One of a recovery workbook series. It guides individuals and clients to understand enabling behaviors and evaluate their current participation in perpetuating the addict's illness. The enabler will learn to recognize the cycle of enabling, entanglement, excuses and beliefs that handicap an enabler from recovery. It also coaches in the courage needed for detaching from destructive people and circumstances we cannot control. The book includes an enabler's recovery plan, accountability questionnaire, self-care program and a plan for identifying unhealthy and healthy coping strategies. It will also guide the recovering enabler to determine a level of safe involvement with an individual with Substance Use Disorder and how to identify true and false recovery, rebuild trust, and avoid the snare of another enabling relationship. It will help us recognize dysfunctional thinking and our false belief system that keeps us entangled. There are 5 chapters from the original *A Thousand Tears*: *Enabler's Journey* book and 3 extra in-depth recovery chapters and many added self-evaluation charts. This is a beginner book for an Enabler. It is short and concise with lots of diagrams and easy to understand flow charts. It is a great beginner tool with lots of reflective questions for counsellors or small groups to use in guiding enablers to recovery.

JOURNAL NOTES

Angie G Meadows MS, RN; Perry Meadows MD, JD; & Sarah Meadows BS